VOLUME 1

A PRESCHOOL MADE FOR PRAISE

Companion Products:

Leader's Guide 0-7673-9668-5
Contains teaching materials, video, listening cassette, listening CD, activity book,
printed piano accompaniment, split-track accompaniment cassette
and split-track accompaniment CD

Listening Cassette 0-7673-9721-5
(available at a reduced price when bought in quantities of 10)

Listening CD 0-7673-9722-3
(available at a reduced price when bought in quantities of 10)

Cassette Promo Pak 0-7673-9651-0

CD Promo Pak 0-7673-9662-6

Child's Activity Bag 0-6330-3564-5
Contains an activity book, crayons, and a listening cassette

A division of Genevox

ISBN 0-7673-9636-7

I Love Livin' Medley

Arranged by C. Barny Robertson
and Anita Wagoner

1 *Shuffle* (♩ = ca. 120)

*I love liv-in' in the love of the Lord, the

love of the Lord, the love of the Lord. I love liv-in' in the

love of the Lord, And the Lord loves liv-in' in me!

**Oh, how I love Jesus.
Oh, how I love Jesus.
Oh, how I love Jesus,
because He first loved me.

*"I Love Livin' in the Love of the Lord," Words and music by JANET McMAHAN-WILSON and TOM McBRYDE
**"Oh, How I Love Jesus," Words by FREDERICK WHITFIELD. Music Anonymous.

I Love Livin'
in the Love of the Lord

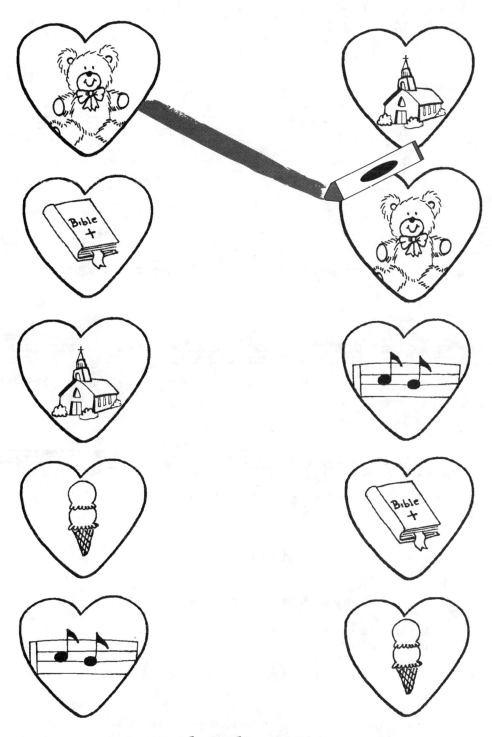

Match the correct
hearts together.

Shake, Shake, Shake, Hallelujah!

Words and Music by
BEN RYAN
Arranged by C. Barny Robertson

Shake, shake, shake, hal - le - lu - jah! Ev - 'ry-bod - y shake!

Shake, shake, shake, hal - le - lu - jah! Serve the Lord, He's great.

Shake, shake, shake, hal - le - lu - jah! Ev - 'ry-bod - y shout! Hey! When

love finds you what can you do ___ but shake, shake, hal - le - lu - jah!

1. When love is in your hand, pass it around.
   When love is in your feet, walk it around.
   When love is in your voice, sing it out!
   When love is in your heart you've got to shake it all about!

2. When love is in your eyes, see for the Lord.
   When love is in your ears, hear for the Lord.
   When love is in your voice, sing it out!
   When love is in your heart you've got to shake it all about!

Shake, Shake, Shake, Hallelujah!

Circle the instruments
you play by shaking.
Put a square around instruments
you play by striking.

Love One Another

Words and Music by
KATHIE HILL
Arranged by C. Barny Robertson

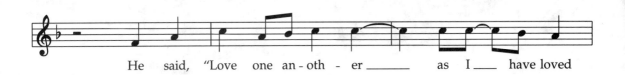

"Love one an-oth-er," He said, "Love one an-oth-er."

He said, "Love one an-oth-er _____ as I ___ have loved

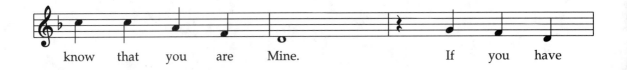

you." "By this shall all men

know that you are Mine. If you have

love for one an-oth-er all the time."

SPEAKER 1: "Whoever loves God must also love his brother." 1 John 4:21
SPEAKER 2: "Love your neighbor as yourself." James 2:8
SPEAKER 3: "May the Lord make your love increase and overflow for each other."
           1 Thessalonians 3:12
SPEAKER 4: "Keep on loving each other as brothers." Hebrews 13:1

Love One Another

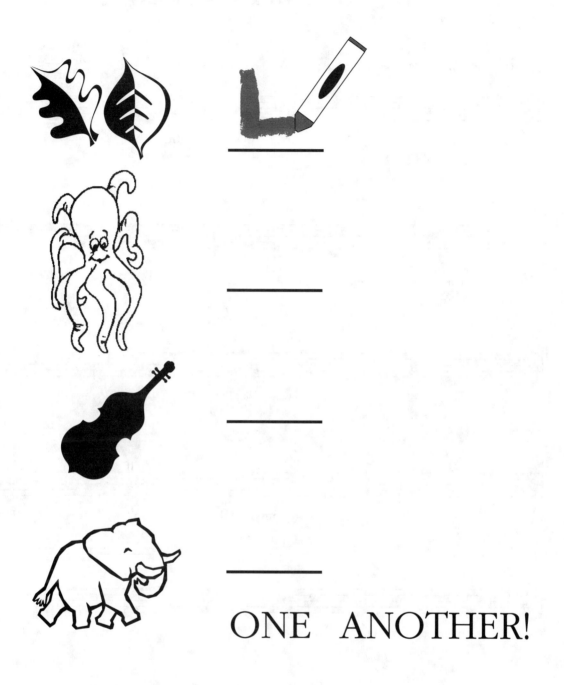

_____

_____

_____

_____

ONE ANOTHER!

Fill in the blank
with the beginning letter
of each picture.

Put Together with Love

Words and Music by
MELODY MORRIS
Arranged by C. Barny Robertson

1. Two eyes, two ears, one mouth, one nose, A
2. Two arms, two legs, two hands, two feet, A

head full of hair, ten __ fin-gers and toes. }
voice made to sing and a smile __ so sweet. }
I was put to-geth-er with

love, Yes, I was put to-geth-er with love.

God's love, there's no mis-tak-in' God's love, It's

worth the tak-in'. I was put to-geth-er with

love, Yes, I was put to-geth-er with love.

Put Together with Love

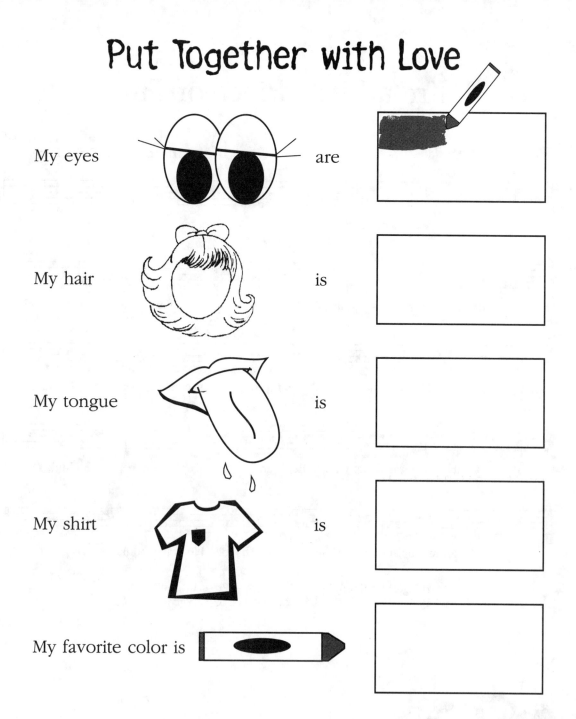

My eyes ... are

My hair ... is

My tongue ... is

My shirt ... is

My favorite color is

"I was put together with love!"

Fill in the box with a color.

I'm a Little Piece of Tin

Words and Music Traditional
Arranged by C. Barny Robertson

I'm a lit-tle piece of tin, No one knows what shape I'm in.

Got four wheels and a run-nin' board. I'm a four-wheel,

I'm a Ford. Honk, honk, rat-tle, rat-tle, rat-tle, crash, beep, beep! Honk,

honk, rat-tle, rat-tle, rat-tle, crash, beep, beep! Honk,

honk, rat-tle, rat-tle, rat-tle, crash, beep, beep! Honk, honk!

I'm a Little Piece of Tin

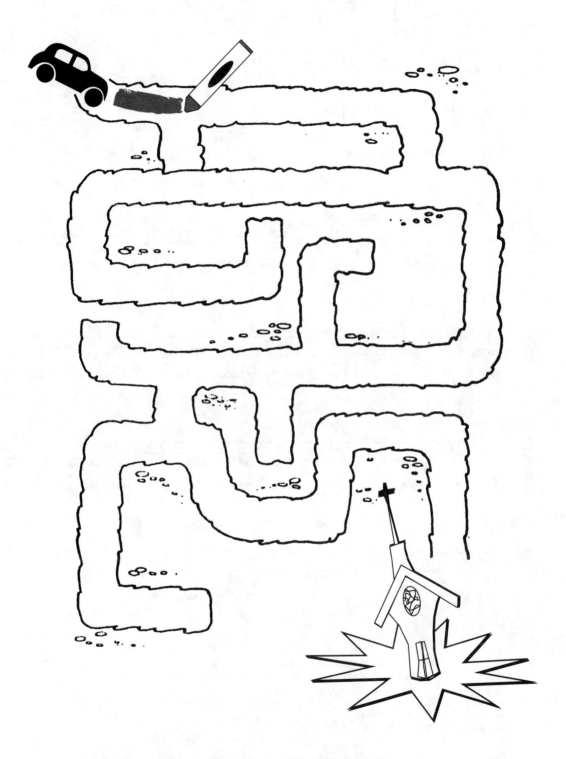

Drive your family's car to church!

Your Neighbor Is the One Who Needs Your Love!

Words and Music by
ANITA WAGONER
Arranged by C. Barny Robertson

Peo-ple all a-round us, pass-in' by, __ Need-in' a friend, I

don't know why. __ I guess God made us all to love each

oth - er. Take the time to share a lit - tle love and

joy to - day, __ As you trav - el on your way, __ Your

neigh - bor is the one who needs your love.

*Someone's cryin', Lord, kum ba yah.
Someone's cryin', Lord, kum ba yah.
Someone's cryin', Lord, kum ba yah.
Oh, Lord, kum ba yah.

*"Kum ba yah," Words and music Traditional.

Your Neighbor Is the One Who Needs Your Love!

Match the pictures that go together.

Friends Love One Another

Words and Music by
CAROL McCLURE
Arranged by C. Barny Robertson

Bright shuffle (♩ = ca. 144)

mf (sung first and third times, play kazoos second time)

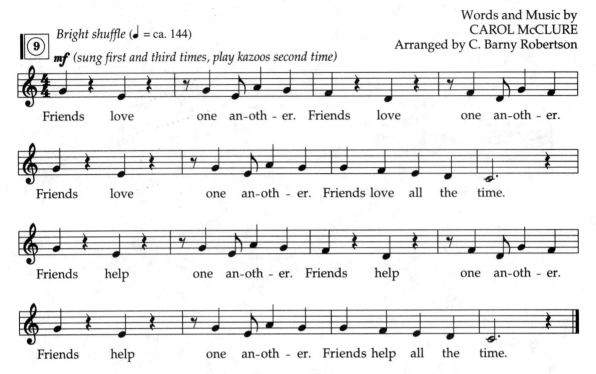

Friends love one an-oth-er. Friends love one an-oth-er.

Friends love one an-oth-er. Friends love all the time.

Friends help one an-oth-er. Friends help one an-oth-er.

Friends help one an-oth-er. Friends help all the time.

Friends Love One Another

Draw a line from the children who are doing good to the smiley face in the middle.

Do unto Others

Words and Music by
ANITA WAGONER
Arranged by C. Barny Robertson

Do unto Others

Color the friend helping.

Do Right

Words and Music by
JANET McMAHAN-WILSON and TOM McBRYDE
Arranged by C. Barny Robertson

Spoken: I can help, I can share, I can tell the truth!

Do Right

Put an X over the children who are not doing right.

Happy Birthday, Baby Jesus

Words and Music by
MOLLY-ANN LEIKIN and CLARK GASSMAN
Arranged by C. Barny Robertson

Hap - py birth-day, Ba - by Je - sus. E - ven when Your birth - day's __ through. All year long we'll re - mem - ber, Each pre - cious gift we get from You. So we sing fa, la, la, la, __ Fa, la, la, la, la. __ He was born on Christ - mas Day. So we sing fa, la, la, la, __ Fa, la, la, la, la. __ He brings so much joy our way.

Happy Birthday, Baby Jesus

Whose birthday is it?
Color the letters that have
a candle in them to see!

Jesus Was the Present

Words and Music by
PAM NOEL
Arranged by C. Barny Robertson

To Us, From God

Connect the dots
to see the present.

Little Bitty Baby

Words and Music by
NANCY GORDON and RHONDA SCELSI
Arranged by C. Barny Robertson
and Anita Wagoner

Lit - tle bit - ty Ba - by. Lit - tle bit - ty Ba - by.

Sleep - ing on the hay. Sleep - ing on the hay.

Je - sus is now with us. Je - sus is now with us.

Born on Christ - mas Day. Born on Christ - mas Day. God's own Son,

sleep-ing on the hay. Pre - cious Sav - ior, born on Christ-mas Day.

Little Bitty Baby

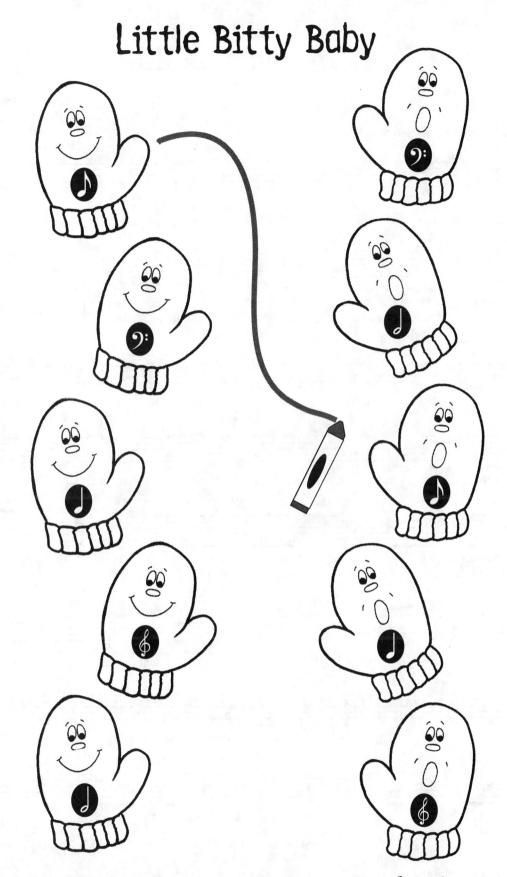

Match the music symbols.

I'm Just a Child

Words and Music by
ED SEABOUGH and TERRY KIRKLAND
Arranged by C. Barny Robertson
and Anita Wagoner

I'm Just a Child

Show how they grow!

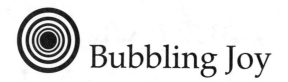

Bubbling Joy

Words and Music by
NANCY GORDON and RHONDA SCELSI
Arranged by C. Barny Robertson

17 *Fun!* (♩ = ca. 116)

mf

It's bub-bl-in' up, It's bub-bl-in' down, It's bub-bl-in', bub-bl-in' all a-round. It's bub-bl-in' in, It's bub-bl-in' out, It's bub-bl-in' all a-bout.

And it's Your joy, joy, Your bubblin' joy in my heart today.
Your joy, joy, Your bubblin' joy, I want to sing Your praise.

And it's Your joy, joy, Your bubblin' joy that will make me strong.
And I can have Your bubblin' joy, bubblin' all day long.

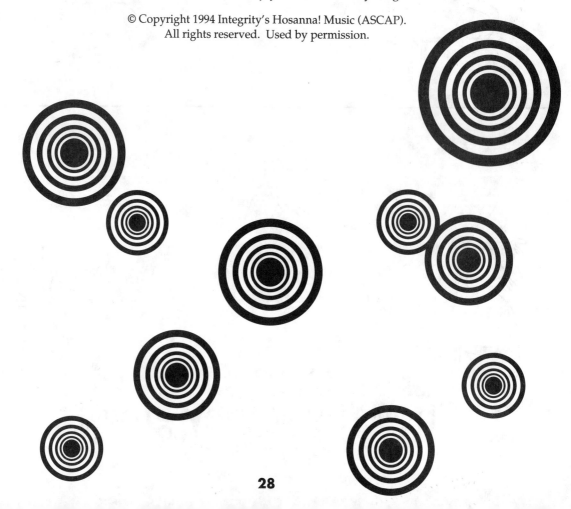

Bubbling Joy

Match the objects that go together.

Jump Up for Joy and Shout!

Words and Music by
ANITA WAGONER
Arranged by C. Barny Robertson

Jump Up for Joy and Shout!

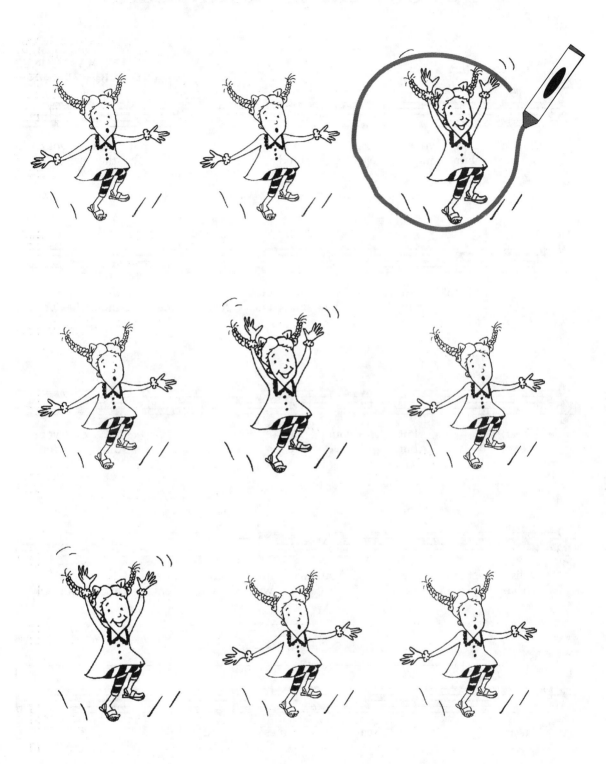

Which one is different?

Put on Your List'nin' Ears

Words and Music by
ANITA WAGONER
Arranged by C. Barny Robertson

19 *In strict rhythm* (♩ = ca. 104)

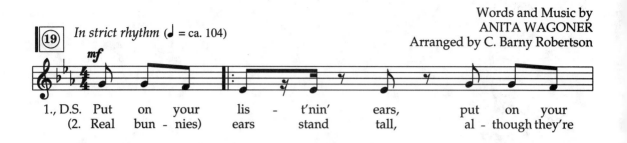

1., D.S. Put on your lis - t'nin' ears, put on your
(2. Real bun - nies) ears stand tall, al - though they're

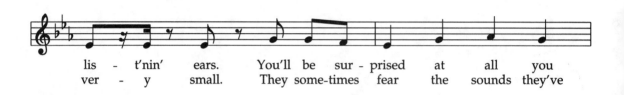

lis - t'nin' ears. You'll be sur - prised at all you
ver - y small. They some-times fear the sounds they've

hear. Put on your lis - t'nin' ears, put on your
heard. But we have peo - ple ears. And we don't

lis - t'nin' ears. You will find out that God is
have to fear if we will lis - ten to God's

near. Real bun - nies Word.

Put on Your List'nin' Ears

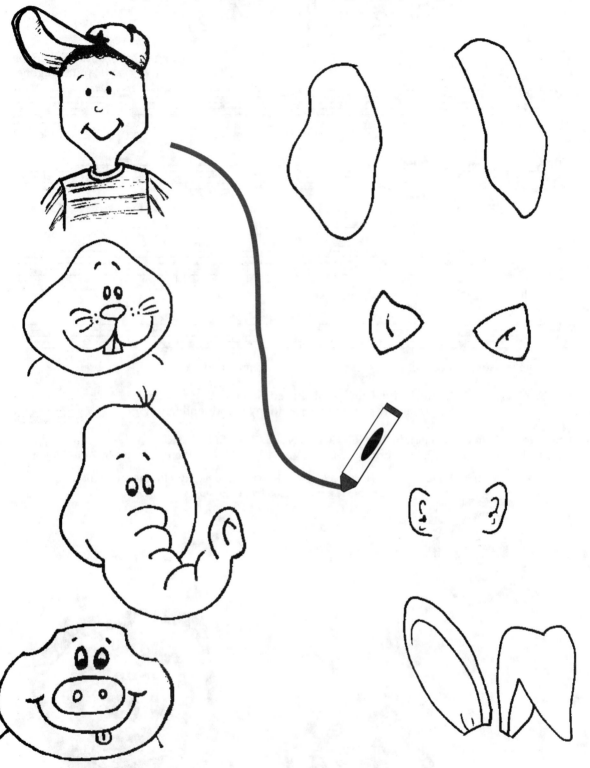

Match the heads with the right set of ears.

Sing for Joy Medley

20 *With strength* (♩ = ca. 126)

Arranged by C. Barny Robertson
and Anita Wagoner

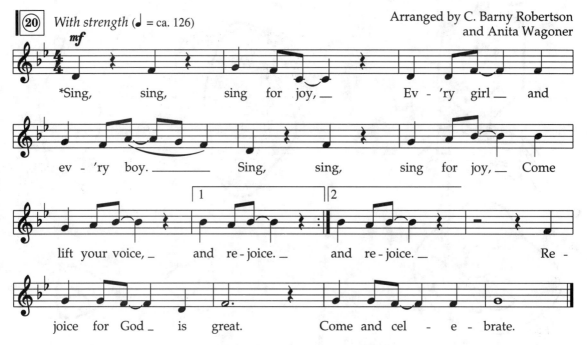

*Sing, sing, sing for joy, — Ev-'ry girl — and ev-'ry boy. _____ Sing, sing, sing for joy, — Come lift your voice, _ and re-joice. _ [1] and re-joice. _ [2] Re-joice for God _ is great. Come and cel-e-brate.

*Joyful, joyful, I am joyful. I'm so glad that God made me.
I will sing my joyful praises with my friends and family.

*"Sing for Joy," Words and music by NANCY GORDON and CHRIS SPRINGER.
*"Joyful, Joyful, We Adore Thee," Music by LUDWIG VAN BEETHOVEN. Words adapted by Anita Wagoner.

Sing for Joy Medley

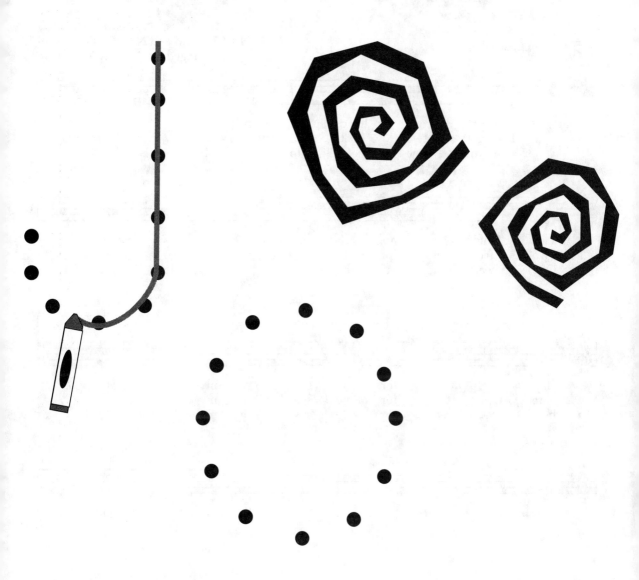

Connect
the dots
to spell a
special word.

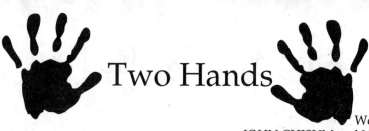

Two Hands

Words and Music by
JOHN CHISUM and NANCY GORDON
Arranged by C. Barny Robertson

1. I've got two hands to clap, clap, clap.
(2. I've got) two feet to tap, tap, tap.
(3. I've got) one heart to beat, beat, beat.

Two hands to clap, clap, clap. Two hands to
Two feet to tap, tap, tap. Two feet to
One heart to beat, beat, beat. One heart to

clap, clap, clap for Je-sus Christ my King. I've got
tap, tap, tap for Je-sus Christ my
beat, beat, beat for Je-sus Christ my

King. I've got one mouth to

sing, sing, sing. One mouth to sing, sing, sing.

One mouth to sing, sing, sing for Je-sus Christ my King.

Two Hands

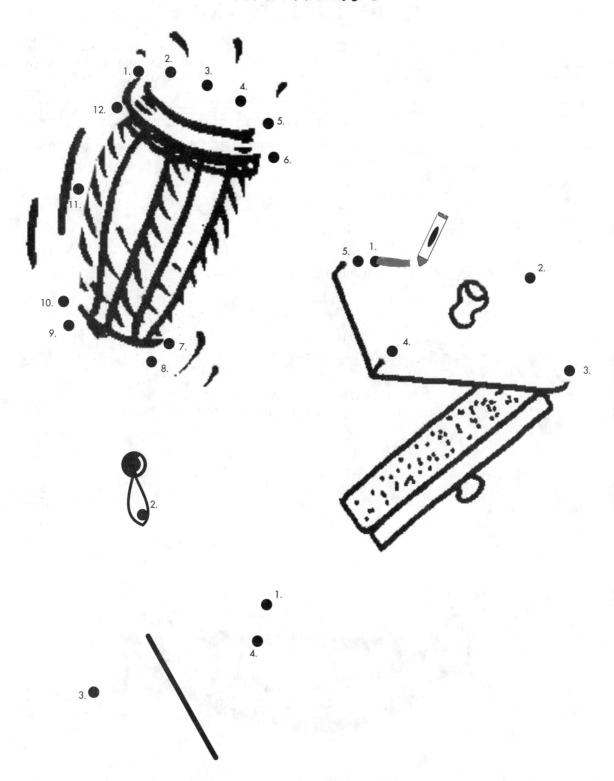

Connect the dots!

Smile, Laugh, Love

Words and Music by
JANET McMAHAN-WILSON and TOM McBRYDE
Arranged by C. Barny Robertson

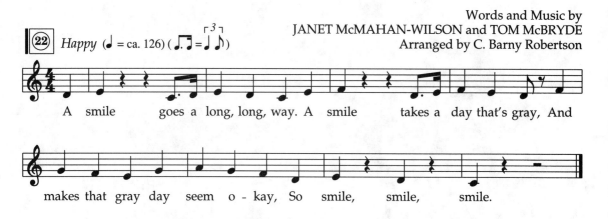

A smile goes a long, long, way. A smile takes a day that's gray, And makes that gray day seem o-kay, So smile, smile, smile.

A laugh goes a long, long way.
A laugh takes a day that's gray,
And makes that gray day seem okay, so laugh, laugh, laugh.

Love goes a long, long way.
Yes, loves takes a day that's gray,
And makes that gray day seem okay, so love, love, love.

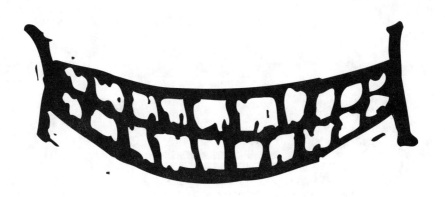

Smile, Laugh, Love

These children are all missing their smiles. Can you draw a smile for each child?

I Was Made to Praise the Lord

Words and Music by
LINDA L. WALKER
Arranged by C. Barny Robertson

With strength (♩ = ca. 126)
First time - CHOIR
(23)
Second time - SOLO

My heart was made __ to love __ Him, __ My voice was made __ to
My hands were made __ to serve __ Him, __ My feet were made __ to

sing to Him. __ I was made __ to wor - ship Him, __
fol - low Him. __ I was made __ to live for Him, __

Both times - CHOIR

I was made _ for the Lord. } I was made _ to
I was made _ for the Lord. }

love the Lord, __ That's what I __ was cre - at - ed for. __

I was made _ to praise the Lord. __ I was made _ for the Lord.

I Was Made to Praise the Lord

Match the object each child is using to praise the Lord.

Music with my friends

Color the Picture!

Watch me grow!

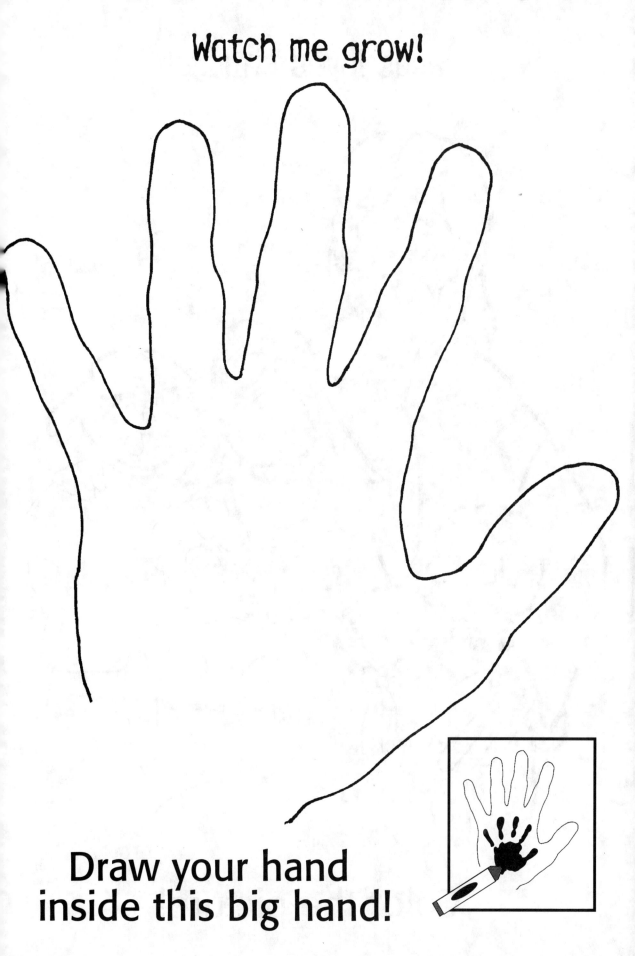

Draw your hand inside this big hand!

Jesus loves children

Color the picture!

My time with God

Color the picture!

Happy Birthday Jesus!

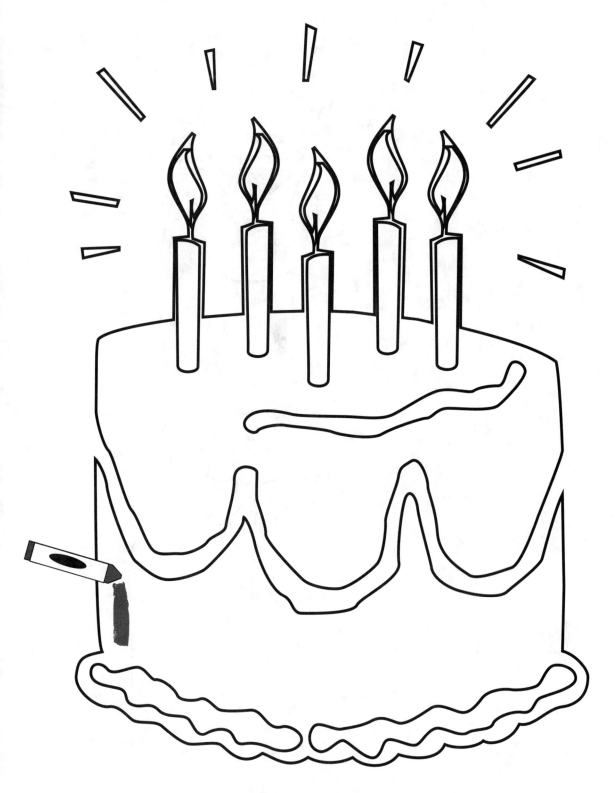

Color the cake!

Jesus gives us Joy!

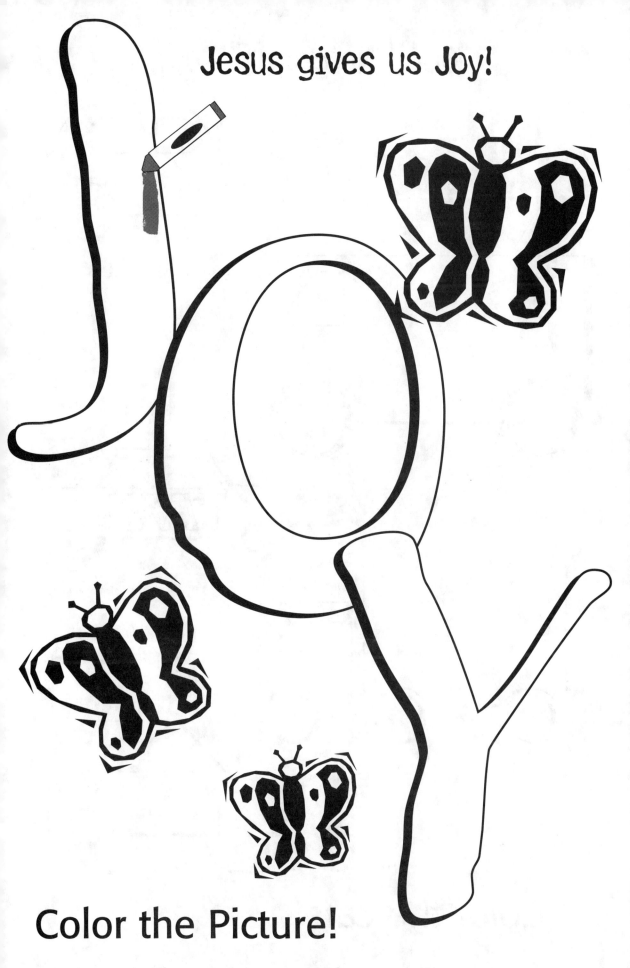

Color the Picture!

"Good Neighbor" Cars

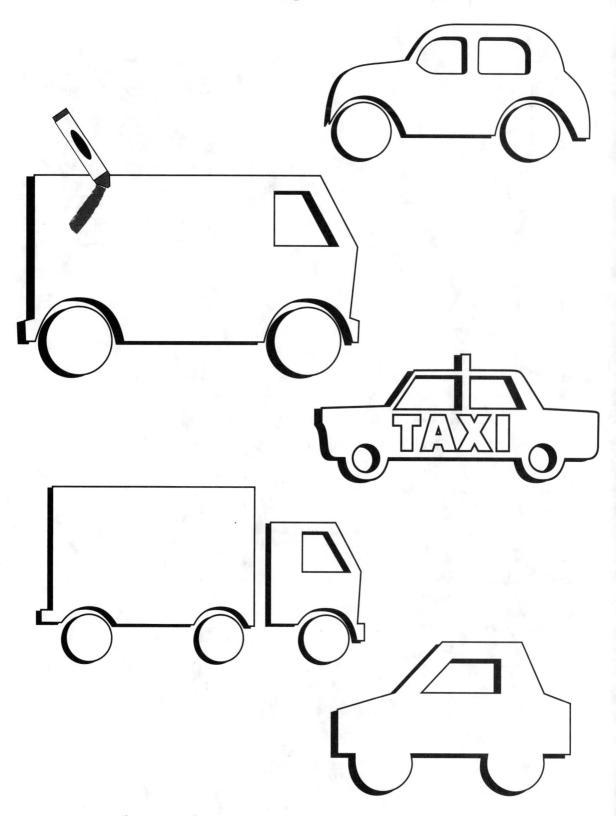

Color the cars!